ATTICIST

Atticist, Ellie Keen Productions,
MAST Mayflower Studios and 45North
present

SAP

by Rafaella Marcus

Sap was first performed at Roundabout @ Summerhall
as part of the Edinburgh Festival Fringe, on 3 August 2022

Sap

by Rafaella Marcus

Cast

Jessica Clark

Rebecca Banatvala

Creative Team

Director **Jessica Lazar**

Producers **David Doyle and Tom Ford for Atticist, Ellie Keel for EKP**

Set and Costume Designer **Rūta Irbīte**

Lighting Designer **David Doyle**

Composer and Sound Designer **Tom Foskett-Barnes**

Movement Director **Jennifer Fletcher**

Stage Manager **Jordan Littlewood**

Production Manager **Lucy Mewis McKerrow**

Associate Director **Charlotte Vickers**

Assistant Producer **Natasha Ketel**

Biographies

Jessica Clark (Performer)

Theatre credits include: the Olivier Award-winning *Rotterdam* (Trafalgar Studios and Theatre503); *Passengers* (Summerhall); *The Funeral Director* (Southwark Playhouse); *The Wife of Willesden* (Kiln Theatre); *The Here and This and Now* (The Drum); *Skin A Cat* (The Bunker and VAULT Festival); *Romeo and Juliet, Merry Wives, Wind in the Willows, The Secret Garden, Macbeth, The Comedy of Errors* (Storyhouse); *The School for Scandal* (Park Theatre); *My Dear I Wanted to Tell You* (Soho Theatre); *Love's Comedy, The Burglar Who Failed, Return to Sender* (Orange Tree); *Respect* (Birmingham Rep); *Be My Baby* (Derby Theatre); *Wild Horses* (Theatre503). Television credits include: *Death in Paradise, Call the Midwife, Silent Witness, Casualty, Doctors, In Search of the Brontës* (BBC); *Versailles* (BBC2/Canal+); *All Creatures Great and Small* (Channel 5); *Broadside* (PBS). Radio and video game credits include: *Kindness* (BBC Radio 4); *Breech* (Bitter Pill) and *Dragon Quest X1; Warhammer: Age of Sigmar* (video games).

Rebecca Banatvala (Performer)

Theatre credits include: *Much Ado About Nothing* (RSC); *Niqabi Ninja* (Toynbee, Lyceum, Tramway); *Mrs Puntilla and Her Man Mutti* (Lyceum); *Rotterdam* (UK tour); *The Three Musketeers* (Dukes); *Deadly Dialogues* (Edinburgh/New York); *Trident Moon* (Finborough). Screen credits include: *The Princess Switch 3, The Syndicate, Love, Death and Robots* and *Emmerdale*. Rebecca is also a writer, currently on the Soho Writers Lab development programme, and makes work with her company Korupt Kabuki.

Rafaella Marcus (Writer)

Rafaella Marcus is a writer, director and dramaturg from South London. As writer, her work for audio includes *The Last Love Song of Suzie Costello* (Big Finish); *Cry Havoc! Ask Questions Later, Trice Forgotten* (Rusty Quill); *The Gift, The You Play: small acts, The You Play Volume II: The Haunted Woman* (45North/Atticist/EKP). *Sap* is her first full-length stage play. Their work as director focuses on new writing, often bringing to the stage marginalised voices. Recent directing credits include: *BLUBBER* (R&D); *Richard II* (RADA); *Stop Kiss* (Above The Stag); *I Have a Mouth and I Will Scream* (VAULT Festival – 2018 People's Choice Award winner); *Bury the Dead* (Finborough Theatre); *Alley. Pearls. Gunshot.* (The Yard); *Spooky Action at a Distance, Crave* (Bunker Theatre); *The Wild Party, The Window/Blank Pages* (The Hope Theatre); *Sonya and Andrey* (Sheffield Theatres); *Laughing Boy* (site specific, Bethnal Green). Work as Associate Director includes: *Blithe Spirit* (Harold Pinter Theatre); *Fury* (Guildhall); *The Cause* (Jermyn Street Theatre). Work as Assistant Director includes: *Emilia* (Vaudeville Theatre); *Pericles* (Shakespeare's Globe); *Romeo and Juliet, The Wind in the Willows* (Chester Performs); *Boeing Boeing, Afterplay, Love Your Soldiers, The Winter's Tale* (Sheffield Theatres); *The Killing of Sister George* (Arts Theatre). Rafaella trained on the Birkbeck Theatre Directing MFA. In 2021, she was awarded an MGCFutures bursary to establish a new free script-reading scheme, supplying essential feedback to writers otherwise unable to access it. They were the runner-up of the JMK Award 2021.

Jessica Lazar (Director)

Jessica is a freelance director and part of award-winning theatre company Atticist. Her productions have won the Carol Tambor Best of Edinburgh Award, the SIT-Up Award for 'social impact theatre', and been nominated for ten Off West End Awards, including Best Director and Best Production. Theatre credits include: Rafaella Marcus's *Sap* (Roundabout @ Summerhall

2022/MAST 2022/VAULT 2020); Lisa D'Amour's *Anna Bella Eema* (Arcola 2019); Iman Qureshi's *this is a love story* and Sam Potter's *Unicorn* (North Wall Arts Centre 2019); David Greig's *Outlying Islands* (King's Head Theatre 2019); Christina Murdock's *Dangerous Giant Animals* (Edinburgh Fringe/United Solo Fest New York/Park Theatre 2018); Steven Berkoff's *East* (King's Head Theatre 2018); and Katherine Rundell's *Life According to Saki* (New York Theatre Workshop Fourth Street Theatre 2017/Edinburgh Fringe 2016). Audio credits include: Margaret Perry's *A Passion Play* and Rafaella Marcus's *The You Play Vols. 1–2* (45North from Written on the Waves series 2020). In 2021/22 she was an ERDF Mercury Creative at Mercury Theatre, and in 2019/20 was an EVOLVE Artist in Residence at Oxford Playhouse. @_jessicalazar www.jessicalazar.co.uk

David Doyle (Producer and Lighting Designer)

David is a freelance lighting designer working across Ireland and the UK. Previous work with Atticist includes: *Life According to Saki*, which won the Carol Tambor Best of Edinburgh Award and transferred Off-Broadway in 2017, *East* at the King's Head Theatre in 2018, for which he was nominated for an Offie for Best Lighting Design, and *Outlying Islands*, which was nominated for an Offie for Best Production. His most recent work with Atticist was *Anna Bella Eema* at the Arcola. Other recent work includes: *Carmen* (King's Head Theatre); *Brendan Galileo for Europe* (UK and Irish tour); *Richard Carpenter is Close to You* (UK and Australian tour); *Dangerous Giant Animals* (Winner of the SIT-Up Award); *The Cat's Mother* (Winner of the Fishamble New Writing Award); *Confirmation* (nominated for the Outburst Award); *My Name is Saoirse* (Winner of the Best Theatre Award at Adelaide Fringe, the First Fortnight Award, and an Argus Angel); *Substance* (Winner of the NSDF Commendation for Lighting Design). His work has been seen in venues across Europe, the USA and Australia, and has been nominated for awards, including the Little Gem Award and the Judge's Choice Award at the Dublin Fringe, and the Edinburgh Award at the Edinburgh Fringe. David also works as a producer for companies including the Abbey Theatre, Ireland's national theatre. He is currently the Resident Producer for Jermyn Street Theatre.

Ellie Keel (Producer)

Ellie is an award-winning theatre producer and the Founder Director of The Women's Prize for Playwriting, a literary prize and campaign for gender equality among writers for the stage in the UK and Ireland. Recent theatre producing credits include: *Reasons You Should(n't) Love Me* (Kiln Theatre and Audible); *You Bury Me* (Lyceum Theatre, Edinburgh, as part of the Edinburgh International Festival); *Collapsible* (HighTide Festival, Bush Theatre, Abbey Theatre and tour); *Redefining Juliet* (Barbican); *Still No Idea* (Traverse Theatre, Southbank Centre and tour); *HOTTER* and *FITTER* (Traverse Theatre, Soho Theatre and tour); and *Anna Bella Eema*, *Mrs Dalloway*, and *Callisto: a queer epic* (all Arcola). As a writer, Ellie is represented by Cathryn Summerhayes at Curtis Brown, and her first novel, *The Four*, will be published by HarperCollins in Spring 2024.

Rūta Irbīte (Set and Costume Designer)

Rūta is a London-based performance designer. She trained in Performance Design and Practice at Central Saint Martins College of Art and Design and was a shortlisted finalist for the Linbury Prize for Stage Design 2013. Her work mainly focuses on devised work and new writing, often in found spaces. Her theatre design work includes: *Say Yes To Tess* (Leeds Playhouse); *Pink Lemonade* and *And the Rest of Me Floats* (Bush Theatre); *HOTTER* and *FITTER* (Soho Theatre); *Slime* (Hull City Libraries); *A New Order* (The Yard); *Primetime* and *Open Court* (Royal Court). In response to the Climate Emergency, Rūta continued her education at the MA Material Futures at Central Saint Martins College of Art and Design, graduating in 2021. She now applies the knowledge and critical thinking gained on the course in her own design practice, and has begun consulting other creatives on regenerative approaches to materials, design and production methods.

Tom Foskett-Barnes (Composer and Sound Designer)

Tom is a composer and sound designer working predominantly in film, theatre and sound art. Film credits include: Academy Award-nominated documentary *Black Sheep* and BAFTA-nominated short *toni_with_an_i*. Theatre credits include: *work.txt* (Soho Theatre); *Anna Bella Eema* (Arcola Theatre); *HOTTER* and *FITTER* (Soho Theatre) and *The Beat of Our Hearts* (Exeter Northcott). In 2016 Tom was Sound and Music Composer in Residence with ROLI as part of the Embedded_Innovate Scheme, and in 2017 Tom was selected as part of the Old Vic 12. Tom trained at the Royal College of Music as a Soirée d'Or Scholar generously supported by a Clifton Parker Award, and was the recipient of a BAFTA UK Scholarship.

Jennifer Fletcher (Movement Director)

Jennifer trained at LABAN and works in a variety of creative roles in theatre, opera and film. She continues to co-direct the two companies she co-founded (The Mostly Everything People and NOVA), who have presented work internationally in Portugal, Spain, Italy, Sweden, Germany and the US. Movement credits include: work for Paines Plough, Theatre Royal Plymouth, National Theatre Wales, Storyhouse, Arcola, Mid Wales Opera, Grosvenor Park Open Air Theatre and The Unicorn. Other roles include, as director: St Just Ordinalia; as associate director: *I am Kevin* (Wildworks); *Don Giovanni* (Longborough Festival Opera) and *Peter Pan* (Storyhouse). Jennifer also co-writes new musicals with composer/writer Harry Blake receiving support/commissions from Andrew Lloyd Webber Foundation, Arts Council England, Hall for Cornwall, the Peggy Ramsay Foundation, The BRIT School, Taunton Brewhouse and North Wall Arts Centre.

Jordan Littlewood (Stage Manager)

Jordan is a recent graduate from the stage management course at the Royal Central School of Speech and Drama. Recent credits include: *The Haunting of Susan A* by Mark Ravenhill, *The Marrige of Alice B.Toklas*, *Thrill Me: The Leopold & Loeb Story*.

Charlotte Vickers (Associate Director)

Charlotte is a director with a particular interest in theatre that explores the world we're living in and the worlds that we might create, and in making the arts themselves a safer and fairer place. Recent directing work includes: *Andromeda* (Camden People's Theatre/Derby Theatre/Nottingham Playhouse); as assistant/associate: *twenty-eight* (Theatre503); *Yellowfin* (Southwark Playhouse). She has workshopped and developed plays at Theatre503, the Young Vic and the White Bear Theatre, trained on the Catalyst programme at the North Wall Arts Centre, and has projects in development with Broccoli Arts and Jessie Anand Productions. She currently works as a fundraiser for national charity Arts Emergency, and is studying for an MA in Gender, Media and Culture at Goldsmiths University.

Natasha Ketel (Assistant Producer)

Natasha is a recent graduate currently working in film development and theatre producing. She previously interned at Jermyn Street Theatre in marketing and producing and has written, produced and directed her own short films, including *Eighteen* and *Model of Life*.

About Atticist

Atticist is a collaborative company founded in 2016, whose distinctive and imaginative work ranges from new writing to revivals with a reason. Atticist's theatre productions include Katherine Rundell's *Life According to Saki* (Edinburgh Festival Fringe/Fourth Street Theatre, New York – winner of the Carol Tambor Best of Edinburgh Award); Steven Berkoff's *East* (King's Head Theatre – nominated for five Off West End Awards, including Best Director and finalist for Best Ensemble); David Greig's *Outlying Islands* (King's Head Theatre – Off West End Awards Nominee for Best Production); and Lisa D'Amour's *Anna Bella Eema* (Arcola Theatre – nominated for three Off West End Awards including Best Ensemble). Audio productions include Margaret Perry's *A Passion Play* starring Nicola Coughlan (part of 45North and EKP's *Written on the Waves* series).

About Ellie Keel Productions

Founded in 2019, Ellie Keel Productions commissions and produces fearlessly imaginative new work for stage and audio. Productions include the multi-award-winning *Collapsible* (Bush Theatre, Abbey Theatre, HighTide Festival and tour); the smash-hit shows *HOTTER* and *FITTER* (Soho Theatre, Traverse Theatre and tour); *Still No Idea* (Traverse Theatre, Southbank Centre and tour); *Reasons You Should(n't) Love Me* (Kiln Theatre and Audible); *You Bury Me* (Edinburgh International Festival); and the critically acclaimed eight-part audio series *Written on the Waves*, in co-production with 45North. In 2022 Ellie Keel Productions was shortlisted for Producer of the Year at The Stage Awards.

Sap

Rafaella Marcus is a writer, director and dramaturg from South London. As writer, her work for audio includes *The Last Love Song of Suzie Costello* (Big Finish); *Cry Havoc! Ask Questions Later*, *Trice Forgotten* (Rusty Quill); *The Gift*, *The You Play: small acts*, *The You Play Volume II: The Haunted Woman* (45North/Atticist/EKP). *Sap* is her first full-length stage play. Their work as director focuses on new writing, often bringing to the stage marginalised voices. Recent directing credits include: *BLUBBER* (R&D); *Richard II* (RADA); *Stop Kiss* (Above The Stag); *I Have a Mouth and I Will Scream* (VAULT Festival – 2018 People's Choice Award winner); *Bury the Dead* (Finborough Theatre); *Alley. Pearls. Gunshot.* (The Yard); *Spooky Action at a Distance*, *Crave* (Bunker Theatre); *The Wild Party*, *The Window/Blank Pages* (The Hope Theatre); *Sonya and Andrey* (Sheffield Theatres); *Laughing Boy* (site specific, Bethnal Green). Work as Associate Director includes: *Blithe Spirit* (Harold Pinter Theatre); *Fury* (Guildhall); *The Cause* (Jermyn Street Theatre). Work as Assistant Director includes: *Emilia* (Vaudeville Theatre); *Pericles* (Shakespeare's Globe); *Romeo and Juliet*, *The Wind in the Willows* (Chester Performs); *Boeing Boeing*, *Afterplay*, *Love Your Soldiers*, *The Winter's Tale* (Sheffield Theatres); *The Killing of Sister George* (Arts Theatre). Rafaella trained on the Birkbeck Theatre Directing MFA. In 2021, she was awarded an MGCFutures bursary to establish a new free script-reading scheme, supplying essential feedback to writers otherwise unable to access it. They were the runner-up of the JMK Award 2021.

RAFAELLA MARCUS

Sap

faber

First published in 2022
by Faber and Faber Limited
74–77 Great Russell Street
London WC1B 3DA

Typeset by Brighton Gray
Printed and bound in the UK by CPI Group (Ltd), Croydon CR0 4YY

With thanks to Hera Lindsay Bird for permission to quote 'Bisexuality'

A CIP record for this book
is available from the British Library

978-0-571-37997-2

2 4 6 8 10 9 7 5 3 1

Acknowledgements

First and dearest thanks to Jessica Lazar for taking a punt on this story when it was still half a script and a collection of bullet points. You understood what this play was from the first moment, and I could not have hoped for a more brilliant and perceptive companion in bringing it to life.

Thank you to Ellie Keel and David Doyle. You championed and stuck by this play when the light at the end of the tunnel for getting to see anything onstage ever again looked so dim and far away. I have been endlessly bolstered by your unwavering support and your understanding of what the play and I needed.

Thank you to my friend Jess Clark, who has been with this play since the beginning, and irrevocably infused it with her deftness, presence, and supreme talent. Thank you also to Rebecca Banatvala, and every other performer who has brought their wisdom and skill to this process at some point along the way, especially Emma D'Arcy, Louisa Hollway and Amanda Wilkin.

Thank you to Tom Foskett-Barnes, David Doyle (again), Rūta Irbīte, Jen Fletcher and Charlotte Vickers: the thought and care you have brought to the development of this play has made it richer and, frankly, cooler than I ever could have imagined.

Thank you to all the friends and family who came to readings, talked with me in depth about their experiences, and generally tolerated me while I navigated the strange waters of writing, but especially to Viviana Marcus (who introduced me to Greek mythology in the first place) and Olivia Marcus.

Thank you to all the scholars, academics, sociologists and generally loud and brilliant voices online who provided me with research into the structural effects of biphobia. Thank you also to the writers, living and dead, whose work guided me while writing; a non-exhaustive list includes Hera Lindsay Bird, Roger Deakin, Charlotte Mew, Carlos Magdalena, Han Kang and, I suppose, Ovid.

And, finally, thank you to David Ralf, who was the earliest reader of this play and the inspiration for many of its most joyful elements. You have never asked me to be anything less than what I am.

Sap was first performed at Roundabout @ Summerhall, as part of the Edinburgh Festival Fringe, on 3 August 2022, with the following cast:

Jessica Clark
Rebecca Banatvala

Director Jessica Lazar
Set and Costume Designer Rūta Irbīte
Lighting Designer David Doyle
Composer and Sound Designer Tom Foskett-Barnes
Movement Director Jennifer Fletcher
Stage Manager Jordan Littlewood
Production Manager Lucy Mewis McKerrow
Associate Director Charlotte Vickers
Producers David Doyle and Tom Ford for Atticist, Ellie Keel for EKP
Assistant Producer Natasha Ketel

Characters

Daphne
a woman, also a nymph; mid-thirties at least

SAP

'It's hard to know what bisexuality means
It just . . . comes over you, like an urban
sandstorm
When a fish crawls up onto land? – that's
bisexuality
It's an ancient sexual amphibiousness

It's like climbing out of a burning building into
too much water
Or climbing out of a burning building . . .
into a second identical burning building
Why does everything have to be so on fire? you
ask yourself
But when you look down, your fretwork is
smoking'

Hera Lindsay Bird, 'Bisexuality'

Note

There is a lot of 'he said'/'she said' in the dialogue sections of this play (literally, not the terrible sexual-assault-trial kind). This is included for ease of reading but can be excised in production if it is sufficiently clear who is saying what.

Descriptions of speech (e.g. 'she says, suddenly alert') may be taken as stage directions.

There is no fixed number of actors that should perform this play.

Dialogue presented in bold indicates words that are spoken aloud, but leaves open the possibility of who says them, the main speaker or someone else. The shift into more traditional play format towards the end is deliberate and should be reflected in production.

*

The play is inspired by the Greek myth of Daphne and Apollo.

This is not to say that anyone watching the play needs to know it's Daphne and Apollo – in fact, the names 'Daphne' and 'Apollo' are never mentioned. But I have referred to the main speaker as 'Daphne' in stage directions and speech prefixes because sometimes the mythic aspect of Daphne makes itself known: the nymph running on the mountainside. How you represent that, if you do at all, is up to you. But it is useful to think of her as Daphne sometimes. Perhaps 'Daphne' is a collective noun: a long line of people who have told this story, or something like it, growing it from the earth like a vine.

Part One

THE BURNING BUILDING

There's a house with trees in it.

I see it from the top deck of the bus to work on Prince's Road, a house with, I swear to god, trees in the upstairs front room. Like someone's ripped out all the floors and planted a forest in the ruins. I think about it a lot, that house, when I'm brushing my teeth or ignoring the phone. The branches battering out the windows and into my head, trunks disappearing down through the storeys, roots cracking the foundations. It's a big forest, I think. Like, if you went in, you wouldn't necessarily find your way back out.

And I mean logically it's just a bunch of overwatered pot plants. A couple of aspidistras, an assortment of japonica, an oversized ficus. It's early. I'm never really awake yet.

I work for a women's aid charity. It's depressing as fuck. I run the Twitter account. Also depressing. Not many followers, but honestly, I get it, no one wants to add domestic violence to their morning scroll. Technically, I'm general admin – the support team, we're called. Because we're supporting the real team, who are running group therapy, and filling out housing applications and someone with actual media training probably should be doing the socials but there's never quite as many staff as there should be, so I end up plugging a lot of holes. (*She finger-guns.*) Ladies.

Okay. I should start with the Lunch. Or no, actually, a morning a week before the Lunch when three important things happen.

Number One. This is the morning, not when I notice the forest in the house, because I'd been noticing that for ages, but when I noticed that no one else could see it. Because I mean we would go past and I would whip my head round at the other passengers like *are you seeing this* and – nothing. No reaction. And, I mean, it's not like it's that surprising that morning commuters aren't particularly awestruck by trees when you're huddled down in the trenches of seven a.m., indoor or not, but still. No one ever saw them.

Number Two. That same morning I make a comment about how pretty the side of the building looks now that it's all covered with that red viney stuff, and Shauna who sits at the opposite desk says **what viney stuff?**

Fuck. I spend the next hour googling plant-based hallucinations. Mostly get a bunch of gap-year kids describing their ayahuasca trips. I'm looking more for something like the bloke that thought his wife was a hat.

And then at lunch I go outside the building and I touch the red viney stuff. It's real. It feels real. And I'm just sort of stroking it and thinking that maybe Shauna just isn't that observant when a bunch of kids on bikes go past and yell at me about wanting to fuck a plant, so I have to immediately emigrate to Australia.

Number Three. This is also the day – I mean it probably wasn't, but it was definitely *around* the same time so look, for the sake of conceptual neatness or whatever, let's just say it was – this is also the day I am invited to the Lunch. Capital L. The Lunches are Miriam from Fundraising's thing, where she takes out companies who are making big donations, and kind of woos them, and then we get more money for beds and shit coffee, and they get tax breaks, so everyone's happy. Miriam is brilliant at this because she's an absolute ten and most of these companies are run by men who say things like 'absolute ten'. Like they're horny but boring about it.

Miriam actually sits on my desk when she asks, which is quite a lot to take in, and she leans forward and says – she smells really good – she says **been meaning to ask, you free for lunch on Friday?** And I feel weirdly nervous when –

I mean for a Lunch lunch, for work – I wanted to say thank you for helping out with my maternity leave. I mean you'd actually be doing me a favour, this lot are deathly and I need someone who can hold up their end of a conversation.

She touches my arm when I agree. **Amazing! Oh, and dress up.**

A pause, a breath.

. . .

The restaurant is cool and dim – West London, of course, nowhere near home or the office. We're meeting a law firm, corporate lawyers who have had some bad PR. Harassment claims – someone quite high up actually got fired, so you know it was bad.

We're sitting school-disco style, the men on one side and us on the other. I'm at the end of the table, rubbing a piece of bread into little pills, wondering when the end of the conversation I'm supposed to be holding up is going to start. I look down the table, and I see –

She is outside the play for a moment. The whole thing threatens to come off its runners. Metal screeching over hydraulics or a shoulder dislocating, but it's also somehow terribly, horribly funny –

She breathes hard. Gathers herself. It stops. Back in.

He's just a guy. Imagine just a guy, and he's exactly what you think of when you think of just a guy. A lawyer-type guy. A good-looking-enough guy. A well-off-enough guy. He probably fucks a lot, high body count, he plays the numbers, he's on Tinder, Hinge and Bumble, hits on women indiscriminately at parties, spreads his nets wide and within a certain metric isn't too fussy about what falls in. When he stands, he'll be shorter than he seems. He's looking at me.

He does a scan across our side of the table. He lingers on Miriam and she winks at him, but easily, like a joke. They must know each other. The other two women are senior staff, over fifty, and his eyes just flicker across them like a barcode scanner. Not rude, just . . . not seeing them. And that leaves me.

The thing is, when someone flirts with you, it's quite hard not to do it back. He holds my gaze a second too long and I dare myself not to look away. He breaks first.

I'm finishing my food faster than anyone else and like a reflex I keep refilling my glass, and I panic in case I look greedy, or drunk, or greedy *and* drunk, but no one's noticing me. They're talking seriously and Miriam is nodding and saying things like **Mmm. So important.**

The lawyer guy catches me looking and mouths **Mmm. So important.** with a really good mimic of Miriam's head tilt, and a laugh shoots out of my mouth. He looks delighted, and I feel bad because Miriam's just doing her job and I know this guy has never for a second set foot in a women's shelter and has no idea what we do, and what the fuck right does he have to make fun of Miriam anyway just for doing her job, which she's good at, and then I remember that I think he knows her as well and it's even weirder to be sharing a joke about Miriam with this guy who knows her, and Jesus, oh my god, fuck this guy.

He must see that on my face because he does a little shrug and turns away to listen to Miriam, and he does seem to be actually listening, he even asks a question which I bet is the kind of bullshit they teach at whatever cloistered quadrangle spat this guy out.

I'm mildly disappointed he's not looking at me any more.

Lunch winds down. We all emerge blinking back onto the street. Spring seems to have happened while we were down there. There's shaking hands and Miriam's happy because they've all but guaranteed a shit-ton of money.

The women are moving back to the tube and I stumble on the pavement and twist like a baby deer in the wheels of an SUV. Miriam catches me. Grins. **Good lunch?**

So good. The food wasn't bad either.

Ugh, I'm so jealous. I'm still not drinking after the baby, not properly, more than one glass knocks me out

I can't help turning back to see if I can catch a glimpse of –

What are you looking for? she says, suddenly alert

Nothing. No one

Aaaaaah she says, with a kind of deep satisfaction. **Of *course***

I don't know what you're talking about

He's such a slut! she cries delightedly. **Good in bed though.**

I roll my eyes but big so she can see. Miriam's gorgeous, but she's never made me wish she wasn't.

Do you want his number? she asks. **Go on, I'm all cooped up with the baby now, it's gathering dust in my phone. Anyway, it was years ago.**

I try to imagine for a moment being the kind of person who would say yes. We didn't even talk. The thought of messaging on the off-chance he wasn't totally repulsed is mortifying.

Alright, well, the offer stands

And when we come back up from the Underground, there is a message on my phone from a number I don't recognise.

What kind of wine do you like?

I hammer a reply quick, and breathing hard.

. . .

She gets ready.

It's a classic mindfuck date. Coffee, but at like five, so could easily roll over into drinks. I realise, too late, that this is what 'taking your look from day to night' is for.

It disconcerts me, this coffee thing, because it implies conversation and – not to be blunt, but this is for sex, right?

Although he did make me laugh. Maybe he wants to make me laugh again. To be honest, who cares, if I'm going to be hungover and sick of myself, I'd rather not do it alone.

He's sitting near the front reading when I arrive, and there's a little tumble of sunlight around him. I feel weirdly grateful for how normal he looks. Then again, I'm reminded of how – attractive, yes, but more than that – *well-groomed* he is. Like he takes care of himself. Which means he probably doesn't *have* to bank on a secluded corner and you not making a fuss, he probably has women queueing up. This leaves me in a bind, as I do want to sleep with him, but I don't want to give him the satisfaction of sleeping with him.

Thanks so much for coming he smiles in a weirdly formal way and gestures to the chair opposite him. Is this an interview, do you want to see my CV, I think.

Do you want to see my CV? I say out loud.

Sorry? he says, pleasantly confused.

No, it just, sounded a bit like you were, interviewing me

Oh I *see*. Hah. Oh, well, in that case, ah, can I ask what attracted you to this position?

I laugh and roll my eyes, which is exactly the response he's looking for.

Well, I think it has some very attractive perks I say. I look studiously at the menu.

Perks?

I shrug. **Free drink.**

He laughs like a bullet, he's delighted. Straight men love that shit: a small joke.

The rest of the conversation goes how I expect, he seems keen to lead and it's no sweat to follow. The way he talks makes me feel keenly thick, like he doesn't just have money, he knows *how* to have money. He namechecks places I've never heard of, restaurants I don't know, in his voice I can hear open doors, travel and art and freedom.

I try to hold up my end but family holidays to Norfolk can't compete. If he'd asked me, I'd have talked about the iron colour of the sea, and the way salt is infused into everything you eat, and the woody, edible smells from the smoking huts, and fish and chips so soaked in vinegar they have to be carefully unpeeled from their paper. I could talk about all of that, but it doesn't feel like there's much point – I don't think I could convince him that the collection of smells and tastes and sounds inside of me amounts to as much as the one inside of him.

The hours have circled the drain quicker than I expected. We've been drinking red, which I don't usually, and I feel flushed. I keep touching my face, and my hair falls over one eye and I must look startled, or sexy, or childish, because he leans over and tucks it back behind my ear. Okay. Here we go.

Do I want this? I want to sleep with him but I don't want to give him the satisfaction of sleeping with him, it clangs again and again in my brain, like one of those logic puzzles, *if a short man enters a lift with an umbrella, what colour was the bear?* I find him attractive, even though I could name a dozen ways in which he isn't.

And then outside the bar he kisses me. And I respond automatically because my body betrays me like that sometimes, like it's just desperate to be close to another warm body and it takes my brain a second to consent.

Tiny pause.

His place is one of those new apartment blocks that are growing like grass in the Docklands – he leads me from the cab through this maze of identical courtyards and building sites, wastelands of rebar like a skeleton forest. **Most of these haven't been sold yet,** he says, **the quiet is amazing** and the empty windows look down at us like a monster with a thousand eyes.

There's foreplay, and it feels a little like an experiment: orgasm is an interesting function of my body, and he wants to know how to entice it out of me. That's not bad, exactly, but it's focused. I'm sensitive and there's a moment when what he's doing tips into being too much, it's uncomfortable, and I try to inch my body ever so slightly to the left, and he holds my thighs even tighter to keep me there. I come anyway, but sort of, fitfully, like it's being dredged out of me.

When he's inside me, my mind slips sideways, and a thought forms: I said Yes, I am saying Yes, but all of a sudden I feel as though I had said No. But I didn't say No. I realise what it is just before he finishes: if I said stop, I don't know if he would. But then it's over, and I'll never have to know.

I do stay the night. I catch a few fretful hours before dawn, when I'm woken by the first rays cracking the blinds. I'm stumbling slightly to get into my clothes when he sits up. In that morning light, he looks soft, softer than he is, his face half in shadow and his hair tousled like a boy's. Something passes through my chest like an ache.

Sneaking out? he says, and I can't catch his tone.

I didn't want to wake you. I say, which isn't an answer.

Do you want – ? He leaves the thought unfinished. He doesn't know what I want.

I'll just call an Uber, if that's okay?

Er, yeah. Course. Do you want – coffee?

So we sit and drink coffee in his clean kitchen, black because he's run out of milk. I want to think that maybe there could be more to this, but there isn't. I can feel the moment slipping away, and neither of us have the energy or the will to call it back.

My Uber arrives, and I want to get into it more than I want to stay. I think it's a relief to him too.

She divests herself of the date.

...

Next week at work the pretty red vines have gone, which is a shame because the building looks like shit without them. I mention it to Shauna but she just shrugs. Maybe she doesn't hear me.

I'm not really waiting for him to call, but every time my phone buzzes a little landmine detonates in my stomach. I'm in Comms. My phone buzzes a lot.

Miriam swings by my desk, **Good weekend** she says, and it's not a question.

Uh yeah. Not bad. You?

Oof, 'not bad'? Not much of a review

I suck in my breath. **Oh, I didn't mean –**

Kidding, I'm kidding. No, I just bumped into him and he mentioned you – saw each other.

Oh, cool. Yeah. We did.

You going to see him again?

Oh. I don't know. I'm not sure it's on the cards, to be honest.

She looks – disappointed? Hurt, even.

Oh. Alright then.

No, he was really great, I just –

No no no, no need to explain. Well. I'll have to think more carefully in future.

I'm still forming the apology as her pencil skirt disappears round the corner.

I wonder what she said to him when she slipped him my number **oh go on give her a call, she'll definitely say yes. Just buy her a couple of drinks.**

I feel sick. Itchy. I want a bath, or a Piriton. An antidote.

. . .

That night, I put on my big black boots and my best jeans and I shovel eyeliner on with a trowel. I'm going out. There's a place I used to go, it's where I've met a few of my –

I actually haven't been for a while.

There used to be proper lesbian bars but they're all Prets now. Still, there's the odd night here and there like this one, that lingered on.

I walk in –

The thing is, I always feel a bit nervous if I'm going to sleep with a woman. I think it's just that I've slept with more men than women because – well, it's just a numbers game, there are more straight men than queer women in the world. And I always want to do a better job with women so it's like – performance anxiety.

I think it's that when I was really young, like, twenty-two, I had this friend, and she was also – she also slept with anyone – I mean, like, any gender. And she was truly like **I just look for a beautiful soul, you know?** But I wasn't like that. I would go out and go **oh yeah, tonight's ladies' night** – and she really didn't like that about me, that I could . . . choose like that.

And then after we started sleeping together, she said I was letting the side down. That I shouldn't let people hear me say those things because they would think I could control it. We didn't want to add fuel to the fire for all the people who thought that being gay, or even a bit gay, was a choice.

And I said well, I'm with you, I want you, I can't control that. Wish I could hahaha.

And she said **you're not with me.**

I did try, I want to be clear, to be – engaged. Political. Because she was really into the idea of The Community – only she never really noticed that she loved The Community much more than The Community loved her. And that was hard to watch.

Did not particularly help me get laid either, wearing my badge that said 'bisexual'. Lesbians find it a bit embarrassing for you, and then outside, in the straight world – the world – you just never have to say it, because it's not a thing anyone ever assumes, it just doesn't occur. So yeah. Being this Out Proud Bisexual just felt a bit juvenile. Making a fuss about nothing. So I stopped calling myself anything.

She's on solid ground now.

I walk into the bar – it's shabbier than I remember, the pleather is fraying on the barstools – and I feel a million years old. I've clearly missed some memos. My jeans shouldn't be tight, I'm wearing too much make-up, my boots aren't fooling anyone, and –

– and when the goddess standing at the bar turns, I see muscles gliding under her skin, and all the breath leaves my body in one go.

She is the absolute queen of My Type. It's almost rude. She's sort of soft and hard at the same time like lipstick on a hammer. She lifts a hand and pushes it back through her hair. How dare she.

For a minute I wonder if she's famous or something because there's a pack of women gathered around her like hunting dogs. I don't even want to try, I came here to feel better not get rejected by Wonder Woman, so I squeeze into a gap and order a drink.

I cannot get over her fucking swagger though. It's sexy but it's a performance. I keep looking over without meaning to and the third time she looks back. Fuck.

For the second time in a week, I dare myself not to look away and, you know what, this time it's easy. She's barely listening to the twelve-year-old purring in her ear, she's looking at me, and I'm looking back at her, and neither of us can keep a straight face. The look is one I know very well. I hadn't realised how much I'd missed it. Direct, and a little bit – hungry.

She gestures to the younger girl and gives an almost imperceptible lift of one shoulder. **What can you do** she's saying.

She's saying that to me! She's saying **what can you do** to me, as though I'll understand, as though I'm like her, someone who people hang off in bars and not someone who hangs. Fuck it, maybe I am.

I give a tiny shrug back – **what a shame you're busy** – and semi-slowly, turn away.

Half a second, and she decides.

She slides out from under the other girl like she's not even there and I think **I've done it, I've won** and she's making her way towards me doing that little bit of a smile, like we're both in on the joke, and it's the best joke of all, and my whole body is waiting for her to arrive.

hi she says, and my fanny hits the fucking floor.

We go to mine. It's closer. It's freezing outside and I go **oh FUCK off**, she laughs a huge laugh, **HAH**

it's ***cold***

yeah? I can fix that and she takes off her jacket and drapes it over my shoulders like some sweet clean-cut jock taking the cheerleader to prom

and I know it can't have but I swear the moonlight softens and warms.

She is still.

That is the night when something slides back, when for a moment I get a glimpse of what my life would be like if I didn't hate myself a little bit all the time. It's like I've been trying to do maths with a number missing.

You are glorious, she said, and I always remember that. Looking back down the long dark lanes of my youth, I don't think anyone had ever called me that.

She's still there in the morning. She stays for coffee, and then she stays for good.

Music; joy.

Part Two

TOO MUCH WATER

anyway every relationship I've had with a bisexual woman She's in full flow, Sunday morning, a month later, and she looks like everything you ever dreamed a Sunday morning would be, **every relationship I've ever had with a bisexual woman they left me for a man or they ended up going out with a man straight after we broke up and after a certain point you're like, well there's a pattern. So I just don't do it anymore, you know? Like I'm not going to put myself through it again. Do you get that?**

The day is still coming into focus and the realisation of what she's saying settles on me like a prickle of heat rash. We haven't talked about exes, we haven't talked about much, it's mostly been fuck-drunk nothings – so she doesn't know I'm – she thinks I'm –

The question she asked is expanding between us like a balloon, any second now it will burst, she will ask why I've gone quiet, so say something, for fuck's sake, say anything,

actually

is what I should say

oh hey hold on

is what I should gently say.

Yeah. Absolutely. is what I say instead, and I laugh. And then the lie is out there. It's out there in the world, and even now it's not too late to call it back, to go **Hey, um, actually I don't know why I said that, the thing is I'm actually**

But I don't.

And the moment goes by, and then another, and then another, and then she's moved on to something else, and already the lie is rapidly cooling into fact.

After that, I self-edit. It's not even really a lie most of the time, I leave things out, anonymise exes, **this one ex used to . . . yeah, they were a nightmare . . .** Mostly I don't bring up my past at all. She seems to like that, like I didn't really exist before she came. A lot of my mates have moved away in the last few years, town got too expensive for hatchbacks and babies, so it's not even a difficult story to keep up.

And the thing is, it's going really, really well. I feel out the places where the swagger ends and she begins, the way she'll pose for photos throwing up ironic peace signs, lift at the gym and light up a fag on her way out, but behind closed doors she melts like butter. Weighs her head on my shoulder like a child. We are going somewhere that I'm not sure I can come back from.

But just every so often she says something that goes through me like cold water. We hang out with her lesbian circle a lot, her coven – her word, not mine – and one time, one of them has just been dumped. Her girlfriend was seeing a guy behind her back – and my Wonder Woman squeezes her hand and says **oh mate, you're better off without her. You know what I've always said about girls who can't make up their minds.**

And the time when someone asks whether a friend should be allowed to come to lesbian book club now that she's seeing a man, and most of them just laugh but Wonder Woman shrugs and – I mean, she might be joking – but she goes **oh, does she *have* to? I do think we could afford to be a bit stricter, it is *lesbian* book club**

Three months later I still haven't told her.

I wonder if I could just pray, and it would be taken away from me, this – nothingness. This amphibiousness. But even that wouldn't undo things I did, unkiss people I kissed. Unlove people I loved.

The ex-boyfriends have come back into my dreams with a vengeance, haunting my pillow, the old shape of them flickering like a bad bulb. I wake up gasping every time, terrified I've said a name, gripped by guilt which is dark green and slithering. One morning I go to the bathroom to wash my face, and I'm blinking prisms out of my eyes, I look up and –

Breath like a tracheotomy.

– that's not me. In the mirror, I can't explain, but it's not – me. It's got skin like – leather, like scales – like *bark*. It's all growths and tumours and yellow eyes, all mulch and soil and matter – I shut my eyes –

And when I look back, I'm me again.

. . .

We're in Kew Gardens the next Sunday, and I'm still a bit jumpy, seeing faces in every tree like a shit Pocahontas. In fact, I'm so focused on breathing in the damp flannel air of the greenhouse, the neat orderly signs by the lily pond – *water lilies belong to the family nymphaea, water lilies are the oldest flowering plants in the world* –

– that I take a wrong turn without noticing. The path slips off my feet, and I realise instead of crunching gravel, I'm sinking into mud. I've wandered so deep into the glasshouse that I've lost everything, even the anchor of her hand. Even the metal ribs of the walls have gone.

The lily pond has become a lake. One of the pads has flipped over, the underside is – weirdly amphibial, crawling veins like a dissected eye. Lilies are unfolding like fingers, white stars that bleed and bruise, and sink beneath the water. And the trees – this is a greenhouse. There shouldn't be trees.

But there are. Trees limbering in all directions, trunks splintering from trunks like a kaleidoscope. I put my hand on the nearest one and I feel it *pulse*, as though sap could move like blood. I feel it rising in my veins, as if in answer. There is a tide washing through this forest, each of these trees is a river of sap, an ocean that rolls with the beat of my heart and for a moment I feel – whole.

– and then it's too much and I'm drowning, my heart thrashing to meet the beat of these trees, the river is a sticky tide pouring through my head, and I'm choking, amber closing over my lungs, until –

– gravel. Anchor. Strong hands on mine and she's hauling me upright, brushing me off

are you alright? what the fuck just happened?

I'm blinking, it was dark a second ago

you were sort of – wheezing, I didn't know what to –

I breathe into her shoulder. She is the most solid thing.

Sorry I – I don't know what that was. I'm okay. Are you –

yeah, yeah, just. don't scare me like that.

I know it's love because I want to say it all the time. I look at her and it nearly slips out constantly.

Have you done the washing-up?

I love you – I mean, yes.

Do you want to go to the pub?

I love you – I mean, sure.

She eventually says it, because I still can't say it first. We say it a lot.

She loves me. She wants me to meet her family.

. . .

Look she says, and it's weird for her to sound this petulant. **I've got this thing with my family in a couple of weeks. Not a**

***thing*, sorry, a wedding, and it's just . . . both of my parents are going to be there, and it's a bit of a headfuck when they're in the same room. And I think Dad's bringing a girlfriend, which is such a fucking stupid thing to . . . and my siblings don't exactly – *anyway*, I know this is soon, but I was wondering, would you go? With me? I – I need you to go with me. Sorry. I haven't exactly sold it.**

On the day, we drive out of town to this – I shit you not – actual castle. I have been a fantastic girlfriend – I've trawled the relationships subreddit, I've got a stack of excuses for getting her out of awkward conversations, and at least three solid hours of small talk locked and loaded.

Also we look fucking great – I mean, she always does, but her boots match my little jacket, and we're wearing the same necklace. We look like a pair. Like we belong. She catches me eyeing her as we park up in the English Heritage car park, and she gives me her hand without looking. I would know the shape of it instantly, in the dark, like a baby's cry.

I have to tell her.

What is it she says

Not now I say

What – oh shit, she says, glancing through the windshield. **Perfect timing as always.**

There's a man striding towards us from the other end of the car park. The sun's behind him but there's something a bit familiar about the silhouette as we scramble out of the car, the walk, it's like trying to place an actor from a voiceover, and then he gets a bit closer and –

A terrible moment like all the oxygen leaving the room.

He's just a guy. Exactly what you think of when you think of just a guy. A lawyer-type guy. A good-looking-enough guy, a well-off-enough guy, fucks a lot, high body count, plays the numbers, Tinder, Hinge, Bumble, parties, spreads his nets wide and isn't too fussy about what falls in. Shorter than he seems. He's looking at me.

She gives him a slightly aggressive hug and when she pulls away, they're the same height. Not an inch in it.

She turns.

Come and meet my brother

Metal screeching over hydraulics. A shoulder dislocating.

We've met he says

Really? she says

Vertigo; a sucking chest wound that continues through the next section.

Yeah. It was a work thing, wasn't it? At that restaurant? He starts filling her in on the details of the Lunch. It sounds mundane and plausible, which it was.

He's so convincing I almost believe for a second that he's forgotten, or that everything that came after was a dream. But then he catches my eye, and of course, of course it wasn't.

I sit in the toilet cubicle and examine how much I have fucked things from every angle, pinballing between self-hatred and the staggering, the fucking unfair coincidence that the last two people I have fucked turn out to be siblings. If I tell her now that actually I've fucked more than a few men in my life, up to and including her own brother – her brother, her *brother*, her brother, who she doesn't even like –

– and then I go crashing out of the cubicle, because what if *he* tells her, what if he's waiting until I'm not there, which is now, so I have to go, go the fuck now –

The gods are on my side because he's standing by himself – half hidden behind a sunflower arrangement checking his phone. She's buried three aunties deep and doesn't see me come back, so I take the long way round a pillar and make a beeline straight for him.

He looks up.

Hi he says, beautifully neutral.

Hello.

There is a strong chance, a very strong chance, I think suddenly, that he is going to pretend he doesn't know me – doesn't *know* me –

Well, this is hilarious. Tempted to ask her to compare notes.

So no.

I presume she doesn't *know*

No, no – I mean I obviously didn't know until just

I mean it's funny obviously

Is it – funny

Well not ha ha. I mean a bit ha ha, it is objectively a bit funny. Blood is thicker than – well, I won't say what.

He drops the smile.

Look he says ***I'm* not going to tell her.**

Aren't you?

Oh god no, she'd probably castrate me. I mean, look, it's up to you, of course, but as far I'm concerned, there's no need to hurt her. She and I hardly ever see each other. And I'm certainly not interested in getting in between this he gestures **thing.**

Right. Okay. Good. I – agree. Great

Great. Our little secret then. Nice to meet you properly outside of a work event for the first time. And he winks, and shakes my hand and my legs almost buckle.

The relief! Not solved, obviously, not yet, but god, I feel on fire. I feel like I can do anything. I might propose. Might fuck about and quit my job and do everything I ever said I was going to –

I catch her around the waist as she's heading for the bar and kiss her right then and there, and even though her eyes dart around the room, she doesn't pull away.

Where have you been?

All your life or just for the last ten minutes?

She snorts **okay**

Just – talking to your brother

Oh, you poor thing. Let me make it up to you she says, and hands me a glass

Aah, he's all right you know and we cheers, and everything, at least for the moment, is fine.

There is a lot more cheersing, as it turns out. Her family are quite imposing – they're like her, a bit too present, too bright. Arguments erupt with fists slamming on tables and then a minute later they're sloshing more of this clear stuff that smells like turps into glasses and yelling blessings. The groom's family look like they're enjoying themselves, but nervously. Like they've been invited to a dinner party in a tiger enclosure. It's silly but I feel a bit like if I draw too much notice – I might get burned up.

I needn't worry – no one's noticing me, except to pass me another shot of paint-stripper. Buzzing, I stumble to the door for a cigarette – I am giving them up, very slowly, but her uncles are chowing down on fat cigars and it's making my lungs nostalgic.

The fridge-door blast of cold carries in an expensive alcohol smell of cologne. He's out there.

I realise unsteadily that it's actually been quite a few months since I was even near a man. Like I don't work with any, and – and look, obviously I don't mean all men are 1950s whisky and aftershave and never really knowing their fathers – but there's something about the way the particles of his cologne hit some wire in my brain like strumming a harp because something in my unreconstructed caveman brain lights up like a switchboard and goes MAN.

And I think this is what – my friend was talking about, all those years ago, isn't it? I'm doing it again. I'm letting the side down.

I haven't told her yet he quips

Hahahagood. Well . . . don't. Please. Oh my god.

You're fine. I'm not going to tell her.

Good

I'm not!

Good!

Mad though. I mean, what are the odds? He laughs, and I laugh too, because it is mad, and I know I'll have to do something about it eventually, but I just feel a bit sort of helpless and giggly right now, and I'll get to it, I'll get to it –

I mean, you could have gone home with anyone from that lunch

No thanks, they were all about a million years old – do you think so?

It was just a figure of speech –

Yeah, yeah. Obviously

So are you thinking about it?

About what?

Telling her. Only give me a heads up if you do, I want to make sure I'm very far away –

We laugh.

I don't know. Not really, it's – it's complicated. Even *more* complicated than . . .

Sleeping with your girlfriend's brother?

Accidentally sleeping with –

Accidentally –

and before I was going out with

Okay, so. Why is it complicated? You fucked our dad as well?

Wow. Calm down. No, it's just – ugh. Oh god, I'm such a bad girlfriend . . .

What? His eyes are roving all over me

No, I can't really say, I can't, it's not fair

Go on

No

You've started now, don't be a pricktease

Hey

Sorry, horrible word – I apologise

No, I, I shouldn't say

Fine. He says. Don't tell me.

And we stand there looking at each other for like, a long time.

Alright I break first. Alright! It's not even a big deal, it's just – it's funny, actually. Well, not really. But, um. She thinks I'm – well, she doesn't know I'm . . . she doesn't know that I like men. As well. Because I sort of . . . well I didn't lie. But I did kind of . . . let her think that. So yeah. So listen – it's doubly important you don't –

Fuck me, he says. Well, I have to say, I did not see that coming. You stone-cold bitch. He lifts his glass to me in mock salute.

Hey

Although now you mention it, I'm not surprised she might be a bit funny about you swimming in both pools.

There's more than two pools I say, but he's not listening

I mean, I've never known her to bring someone home who wasn't, you know. Just a massive dyke.

I go very still. I can feel something under my feet, like an Underground train going by, but I'm also very drunk, I realise.

Who's better, me or her?

What? I . . .

Me or her? Come on, it's just a bit of fun. Me or her?

I don't – it's not – sorry, I don't really want to answer that.

So it's me

No

So it's her

I uh . . . you can't ask me that

I'm just saying. You clearly already know the answer. I bet I can get you to tell me.

Stop it I say, and I'm trying to laugh but it sounds weak, it cools in the night air.

This is so interesting. You'll have to tell me at some point he says, and vanishes.

Prick, I think. Don't have to tell you shit.

She laughs; she sobers up.

What a fucking idiot. What a –

. . .

I'm tense after the wedding but nothing happens so I think, he was just drunk. It's probably fine.

They've been talking more since the wedding and she's got it into her head that it would be nice to see him again and keeps saying so, quite defensively. One time she goes as far as **Maybe we should have him over for** – and then I change the subject and she's relieved. I try to get out of Miriam if he's seeing anyone so I can relax and that can be the end of it. Because I mean – I definitely can't tell her now.

Maybe that's okay. Maybe I can just – have this.

Beat.

I'm home one evening when the buzzer goes and my housemate yells that it's for me. Wonder Woman messaged a while ago to see if I was in so I'm already reaching for her as I round the banister –

It's not her. Standing in the hall with a bottle of wine. It's him.

I was just in the area he says, **and I thought . . .** He holds out the bottle.

How did you . . .? How did you know where I . . .?

Yeah I was just passing by

What the fuck is happening?

Right.

It's the first time I've seen him out of a suit and he looks . . . good? The sight of him in my kitchen is faintly surreal, so normal, so much like he belongs, foraging a corkscrew and passing me a glass. I wonder for a second if I've fallen sideways into a parallel reality, like the next words out of his mouth are going to be **Darling, shall we go to bed? It's been a day**

I take the wine from his hand automatically.

How'd you get on with the journey back after the wedding? He swills his glass. **Not bad this.**

Fine, yeah, traffic was . . . fine. Look, are you – did you need anything? I mean, did you want, something I can . . .

Does he know she's coming round? *Could* he know that?

No, no. Like I said, just in the area. Thought I'd drop this round.

Okay. Okay, yeah, that's, that's really lovely, and I'd love to – I'm actually a bit – I was sort of winding down, to be honest – I'm so sorry, I wouldn't normally, it's just a bit of an early start in the morning

Oh sure he says smoothly. **God, didn't mean to inconvenience.**

No, no! It was . . . great to see you!

And then I can feel it welling up,

Another time maybe!

He studies me for a long second. **Yeah** he says thoughtfully. **That would be great.**

I don't mention the visit to her. Of course. I wouldn't know how to – there's no context I could fit it in that would make it normal.

And I don't mention it the second time he comes over, or the third, or the fourth. At no point does he touch me. At no point does he do anything other than bring a bottle of wine, nice wine, and drink it with me in the kitchen. And he talks to me. At me. About his job, his colleagues, his gym membership policy. Travel and art and freedom. And when the wine is finished, he leaves, and tells me he looks forward to next time.

I try not being in. Make plans every evening for a week. When I get back, there is a note fixed to the front door. *Sorry to miss you this eve. Maybe I'll call my sister and we can all go for a meal some time?*

Cold water in my guts. The message is clear. And the note is weird, a deliberate choice, he wants me to know that he was standing at my door. I wonder about talking to Miriam but then I think – well, someone gave him my address.

When he next visits, I am very still. We stand facing each other, our backs against the counters in the small kitchen.

He hands me a glass.

No thank you I say.

My sister loves this one he says.

I take it. I sip very small, precise sips. He refills it before it's half-empty.

He's doing another endless spiel about work, a contract –

Maybe you should share this with a friend – if there is – a friend.

Beat.

I'm boring you.

Beat.

How rude of me. You're right, I have been – talking about myself far too much. Tell me about *your* day.

This feels like a trap.

No

Tell me about work, how's Miriam?

I don't think that's –

Your family, I can't remember what you said on our date –

No I think you should just –

Tell me about your relationship with my sister.

—

Or I could just ask her.

I say nothing. He gets out his phone, and holds it up so I can see. I say nothing. He finds her number and shows it to me.

I say nothing.

He presses call, and I say nothing, and it rings for two rings, and I say

okay

He hangs up.

Okay what?

Okay, I – what do you want to know?

I told you. Something about my sister.

She's . . . about five foot –

No. No. Tell me something about her. About being with her.

—

You won't shock me. I've known her my whole life.

. . . she . . . she always says no to milk in her coffee. But then after I've given it to her, she gets up and puts some in.

I know that he says. She's always done that

It – annoys me when she does that. Even though I know it's not my fault, it feels like it's my fault.

Okay. Okay, good. Getting somewhere. What else?

What else – ?

Things that annoy you, what else does she do? I know there's more.

No, she's –

Come ON. I know what she's like. You can say it. She's not perfect.

. . . I suppose . . . sometimes she can be a bit – sometimes I have to repeat myself.

She doesn't listen to you.

No, no, she, she does – it's not just me, it's a general –

She doesn't listen to *anyone*? Yeah that tracks

No, I just mean she doesn't always hear other people the first

It's difficult, isn't it?

I mean she's very decisive, she knows what she wants, she's –

Judgemental

No

Dismissive

No

Controlling

No!

Beat.

I'm sorry. That must be very hard for you.

Silence.

Is she controlling in other ways?

No. How do you mean?

Well. I mean. Who drives?

I – don't have my licence so

No, no. No. Who *drives*?

I –

Does she go down on you? Or do you go down on her?

—

I asked you –

Yes. I heard –

Come on he says, and he chinks his wine glass against mine. Here's to oversharing

I should lie. I should tell him something that's not true.

Both I say instead it's pretty even

Are you good at it? Do you think? I know you haven't had as much practice as her – or I don't know, have you? What are your percentages? Man-woman wise?

—

Don't you just worry you're shit at blow jobs *and* eating pussy?

That's not how it – you can't –

I'm just curious, don't get offended. Do you still fancy men? Or is it muff all the way for you now?

He laughs a laugh like marbles crashing in a tub

No, I'm just joshing. I know you'd fuck anyone.

No, I – I love *her* – I'm with *her*

You know – and this is a secret, but I'm keeping yours so, bit of quid pro quo – it's actually quite hot. That we – and now you're with my sister. I know, bit weird but he shrugs **what can you do? I wonder if I'd even . . . ? Both of you? Probably not**

He sees my face and bursts out laughing again

That was a joke! Oh my god. Learn what a joke is, yeah? Except about it being hot. It is weirdly hot.

Somewhere in this time, he has stepped closer to me. My back is against the counter and I can feel his breath falling on my mouth like rain. My own breathing is hard like I've been running. White tendrils are curling blindly from the kitchen cabinets, trunks are groaning up through the floor, the forest is splintering around me, I need to move but –

A terrible wrenching.

My feet split open. Shards of bark unfold out of me like something prehistoric. Vines are knotting my tendons, cracking my ankle bones, tying me down to the earth. I will stay here for a hundred years, just another tree inside a house who was once a person.

Christ, I better go he says, soft. **Gone midnight** And he leans down and kisses me on the forehead. I don't move for a long time after he goes, maybe not until my calves start to cramp and my knees buckle, and I crawl into bed fully clothed.

After that it gets much, much worse.

He tells me, in detail, about the things that turn him on. Most of these fantasies involve women having sex with other women. Sometimes I am in them. Sometimes I am having sex with a woman who could be her. Sometimes they are threesomes and sometimes in the threesomes he is so good at sex that we forget about having sex with each other and just have sex with him instead. Sometimes he just watches.

He tells me all of this in my kitchen, in my house, and when I try to move, I feel the knots of my legs pull tight. Bark encases me like eczema, scabbing my wrists, blistering the skin of my belly. He texts small, innocuous messages, *just checking in, give me a shout if you need.* As though he's terrified I'll forget him.

One day, his hand undoes his belt while he's talking, like it's the most natural thing in the world. I want to smash his hands with a frying pan, I want to break every little bone in his fingers, plunge them into hot oil before he carries on doing what he's doing. But bark has locked up every knuckle and joint like arthritis, and I can't flinch, let alone pick up a pan.

He does it again, and again, and again. He tells me, with laboured breath, that I like this. That he's giving me something I won't get from her. My roots sink further into the earth, my bones choking in green, my pulse sticky. Bark creeps up my body like a rising sea level. I wonder what will happen when it reaches my heart.

One time I manage to say, and it costs me so much, it's as though I'm swimming slowly towards a surface a long way away

Why are you doing this?

And he looks at me for a long time and says, with perfect sincerity,

Why am I doing what?

. . .

I am splitting into two people, the one who is with her, and the one who stands in the kitchen with him, and I know I won't hold much longer. I think if I really could split in two, a full-body mitosis, that would be the answer to my prayers. Throw half of myself to him like chicken fillets to a crocodile: sacrifice, protection. Payment.

She knows something's up. It would be impossible for her not to. Sometimes when she comes near me in the dark now, her figure, her voice, even the smell of her is a little too familiar, too *similar* and I – she's not making a big thing of it, but I can sense her concern is growing, the question she's not asking me, the bottom of the barrel is coming up fast.

I spoke to my brother on the phone today

—

I said we'd go round for dinner next weekend.

Really? I mean, do you – want to?

Well, we're free. I thought it would be nice.

I – um – we can't next weekend. Hasn't – whatsherface got a poetry night?

Oh shit, yeah. But we never go to those.

Yeah, I mean, that's why, I thought maybe we should.

Ugh. Yeah. Yeah, you're right. Okay, I'll tell him another time.

How did he – I mean, why do you think he asked?

Who knows why he does anything. Maybe he fancies you. She laughs **I mean I can go back to him and suggest another date if you're that keen –**

No! No that's not what I – meant.

Okay.

And then she looks down, and back up at me, and says

You know I love you, don't you?

And I say

I wish you'd check with me before you say yes to stuff.

He texts me later when we're in front of the telly, *Say yes to dinner*

And I text back, *why*

And he says *It'll be funny*

And I say *I don't think it will be funny*

And he says, *Or maybe I should just come round to hers*

And then he texts again, *Is there a particular red you've liked? I'll get some in*

Is there a particular red you've liked? Why am I doing what? I stare down the barrel of this going on and on and on, and I know there are so many more depths for him to plumb, I know there is so much more he wants from me.

I think I thought that somehow this was the price. Not just for the lie, but for something else, something weak and undecided in me. But I see now I am being axed into pieces and told that it is simply my nature.

She's fallen asleep on the sofa. Her hair is fluttering away from her mouth as she breathes, like she's underwater.

I think, water lilies are the oldest flowering plants in the world, water lilies belong to the family *nymphaea*. Like nymphs, like the girls in stories who suffer and change. I think of all those water lilies, waiting for millions of years below the surface. All those drowned girls waiting to come back up.

I text back. *Okay.*

Part Three

WHY DOES EVERYTHING HAVE TO BE SO ON FIRE?

The following weekend I travel alone to his flat. I've told her I'm not well enough for the poetry reading, and the lie comes so easily to me. This time I'm bringing the wine.

Just like the first time, his is the only light on in a block of a hundred flats. Just like the first time, the courtyards are an endless sterile maze, and I feel contempt that he would choose to live here. Good.

When I ring the buzzer, I say **It's us** and he buzzes me in, and in the lift up I'm almost excited. He opens the door and when he finds only me, he's knocked off balance.

Wine? I ask, and push my way in. I pour him a large glass of red, brimming.

I think we need to have a chat I say, and I am scared, so monstrously scared.

Where's –

She couldn't make it.

So why are you – ? You never told her.

The table is laid for three, there are cloth napkins and candles like it's a date. From the window I can see the river, and I wonder who's down there, how many.

You're going to stop coming to see me.

Sorry?

I think you heard.

I don't understand.

I don't like it. Stop coming.

It's just a bit of fun.

No, it's not fun. It's bad. It's sick.

I think that's an overreac—

It's a crime. You're a criminal.

He stares at me, then goes for his phone, **I should call her. Just to let her know you're here, let her know you're safe.**

You can try I say, and a shake is creeping up my left leg but it hasn't reached my hand yet, it's steady as I hold up her phone but you won't reach her.

He dials anyway, and watches it light up in my hand. I turn it off.

So now we can talk uninterrupted.

He gulps back a slug of wine and a little trickles out.

Go on then. Say your piece.

I want you –

Well, I know *that* –

To leave me alone.

Beat.

Do you?

Yes.

No, I mean, it's just – I'll miss you.

—

And then I might have to come round and see you both –

Stop it.

Oh, maybe you're right.

Am I?

Maybe we should just make a clean breast of all this. Sit her down and tell her the truth –

If you tell her, what do you have left?

Pause.

I don't . . . where did this come from?

He says my name and it's almost tender. I want to claw my own skin off.

Why do you want to stop? You've got the best of both worlds here, much better than I do, sitting all alone here in this silly flat – it's not even like you're really cheating on her –

What the fuck are you talking about

I think we've got a real connection, are you telling me you don't –

We don't have a *connection*. Do you really not know – what this is –

And for a moment I almost believe that.

Bullshit. I say **Of course you know. Of course you do. You're a rapist.**

His blokey, baffled, mea culpa ease drops like a stone

No, hey, hang on, that's not, that's not what – how fucking dare you

He's shaking.

You know what, forget it, it's just a shame, you know, it's a waste. I was trying to help you and if you saw that, I think you'd be happier. I was trying to help you, help you realise –

A high vibration like a glass about to splinter.

What were you going to do when it was over anyway? This little lezzie adventure? Go back to men. I was just trying to help you get there, and if you had a moment's honesty, you'd admit –

If you come near me, I will tell her what you've done

Shit. I've made a mistake.

Ah. That's what this is all about, isn't it. Coming here. Coming to see me and not her. Go on then. Tell her.

Beat.

You won't, will you? Pretending you're the victim. Like you didn't choose to come here, like you didn't bring me fucking – *wine*. You make me sick. Don't! – look at the door, she's not here, she's not going to –

Beat.

She doesn't know you're here. And if you've got her phone, you can't tell her where you are.

And he goes for me.

Something alters in the state of the world, like tearing down a curtain and finding rooms you didn't know were there.

You know what happens next. Because it's what happens. It's what always happens.

I've tried so many things at this point. I've tried refusing to do it. I've tried standing there with my arms crossed and saying 'no, it's boring, not doing it'. I've tried walking away. I've tried doing something else, demanding to be allowed to do something else, slay a monster, or seduce a sorceress, or descend to the underworld, but

in the end, this is the story where this happens. Is happening. Has never stopped.

In a Docklands apartment, a man is moving across a room towards a woman, and on a mountainside a god is moving towards a nymph, and I can slow it down and walk around it but I can't stop it.

Before it happens I want you to know that this is not the point. It's not the point of me.

I'll try to make it quick.

The world snaps back.

He goes for me and I crash into the table. Everything shatters and gives me time to roll away and I feel her phone crunch in my pocket. There's glass in my hand and my side, but I scrabble across the floor, he grabs my leg and I kick out behind me. Cartilage crunches and there's blood. He calls me a bitch, and I claw the front door open and I run. I pelt down five flights before I lose my footing and fall the remaining two. The station is a fifteen-minute walk, I'm limping, I don't know if I'll get there, I've left my phone and my purse, I am completely, completely alone.

I can't remember the way I came in. There's half a dozen identical alleys leading to other courtyards and none apparently that lead to the road. Behind me in the entrance a light goes on.

I just run. I run blindly, I don't know where I'm going, I don't know what leads to where, so I just try and shake him. The wound in my side is sending little waves of pain down my leg and I'm crying and I can't tell if the lights in my eyes are me or the thousands of windows.

He's gaining, I can hear him. I run until I am in the building site, I am on the mountainside. I'm tripping on the uneven ground, I'm dodging trees, rocks, fingers of rebar that jut from the earth. It's so quiet, we could be the only two people in the world. I trip one too many times, and when I try to stand I can't. I crawl behind a little bank of soil and wait. If I can just sit here, if I can just hide long enough. Morning will break, and someone will send me home and put me to bed.

But then I hear him, taking his slow time, because he knows this is it. Can't run. Nowhere to hide. I tilt my head. There's a thin, watery moon, but there are no stars, or maybe there are thousands.

So I say her name, because wherever she is I want her to know that I'm sorry. For the lies, and – for not running fast enough.

I know she says, and she sounds so sad. She's silver in this light.

Help me. I don't think I deserve this, and if you can help me –

The deep bone-wrapped pain is starting, the tendrils climbing to choke my legs

No, not now

Stand up she says, and I don't know if it's her or just me talking to myself. **You have to meet what's coming**

She reaches down and touches my wrist where my pulse flickers. My pulse that is filling with gold.

She touches Daphne's wrist.

It will rise to meet this.

All of it?

All of it.

She pulls me to my feet, I'm getting to my feet, my feet are on the ground, my feet are *in* the ground, I turn to face him –

And then. My miracle happens.

I plant my feet in the earth and there and then, they take root. The crevices in my skin turn dark and hard and the bark that's always there wells up from beneath the surface, tearing aside my skin. Shoots erupt from beneath my fingernails and they split and fall away. My torso twists as my spine fills with lignin, stretches, stiffens, grows.

It hurts. I'm gasping for breath as the wood pours through my chest; tissue changes, cells rewrite, my lungs collapse, my liver petrifies, and my hair blooms from my scalp like a mushroom cloud. And then the river of sap washes through my body and I can breathe, my heart drums as the bark closes over my mouth, *it's me, it's me, it's me.*

When he arrives into the glade, his excitement wafting like pollen, he sees a tree. I look down at him from the new metres of my body.

He places a hand on my trunk. On one side of the bark, his hand. On the other, my heart. All I hear is silence. Nothing but the sound of my own leaves.

. . .

When I turn up on her doorstep, she insists on taking me to A&E because there is glass in my side and I'm bleeding and won't speak. She's been going spare because she couldn't find her phone, and when I hand it over broken she looks at me and goes **what the *fuck's* been going on?**

She drives me to hospital, and they whisk me away and patch me up – it wasn't a deep wound – but they are more concerned about the way I won't speak, and they keep asking me questions. A nurse very gently looks past me to my Wonder Woman and asks if everything's okay, and when I crumple, she drops her voice even further and says they do have people I can talk to, they can do a rape kit – I shake my head. They're busy, of course, and relieved to let me go.

But when we get home, she has questions. She thinks – a stranger – unlucky – and I could let her.

Breath. Head down. Breath. Head back up.

It's a strange thing, to come out to your girlfriend. After the dirt washed off my tongue, over days and weeks, and shock turned into – something else. I'll say this for her, she was very precise, very slow and deliberate and –

Her Don't do that. Just talk to me.

Daphne turns to look at her. She is more real than she's ever been. Daphne tries to talk. Really tries. Crumples. She rushes to Daphne and holds her.

I'm so sorry I'm so sorry I'm so sorry

Daphne No I'm sorry

Her What the fuck are you – don't you dare apologise

Daphne No but if I hadn't

Her If you hadn't bullshit, he did this, he did this, and I'll never, I'll kill him

Daphne what what what are we going to do –

The scene resets.

Her Don't do that. Just talk to me.

Daphne Sorry.

Her I imagine you are sorry now, yeah.

Beat.

What, bit victim-blamey was that?

Beat.

Sorry.

Daphne I know I shouldn't have – I shouldn't have lied.

Her No shit. Okay, well, I think we can take that as a given. So?

Daphne So . . .?

Her So – fucksake, you know what I'm trying to ask – so – how much was true?

Daphne Of what?

She gestures: 'All of it.'

Of what I told you . . . most of it. Kind of.

Her Kind of. Okay. How many?

Daphne How many what?

Her How many men? I'm just trying to get a sense of –

Daphne Of what, of how gay I am?

Her Yeah, kind of!

Beat.

Daphne I don't want to do this.

Her What *do* you want to do?

Scene resets.

Don't do that. Just talk to me.

Daphne It's difficult

Her Well . . . try. I think a little bit of effort –

Daphne Yes. You're right. Okay. So. So . . .

Her Shall we start with *why*?

Daphne I don't know.

Her Please.

Daphne I – okay. I didn't want to lose you. You're the best thing I ever – I love you so much and

Her I love you. And what?

Daphne —

Her I was going to spend a lifetime with you.

Daphne Don't say that. We can still

Her Were you ever going to tell me?

Daphne —

Her Were you?

Daphne I don't think so, no.

Her Well. That's that then.

Beat.

I can't be with someone who doesn't want to be what they are.

Daphne But you don't like who I am. All that stuff about 'I don't fuck girls who can't make up their minds, it's not worth the hassle' –

Her Honestly, who gives a fuck what I like?

Daphne I do.

Her Yeah. Bit of a catch-22 that, isn't it.

Silence.

Daphne So . . . what do you want to –

Scene resets. They are very tired.

Can I talk to you?

Her What more could there be to say?

Daphne I –

Her No, I mean it. You talk endlessly, on and on and on, your fucking deluge, your fucking biblical fucking flood of words . . .

Daphne Sorry. I won't then. I'll stop.

Her Please don't.

Beat.

Please keep talking.

Daphne I thought –

Her I don't want to get to the end of this conversation.

Beat.

Daphne Me neither.

Her Maybe as long as you keep – spouting bullshit

Daphne Hey

Her We can just . . . Please keep talking.

They look at each other for, like, a long time.

Daphne Don't know what to say.

She leaves.

It's not that those things didn't happen. They just didn't *all* happen.

If there was some magic combination of words that unlocked the right ending, like a video game, like a choose-your-own-adventure, like the Do-Re-Mi of a perfect string of notes dropping one by one into your heart forever –

But there wasn't that.

In the end, there was just me, feeling very small and cold and – *embarrassed* and saying **well, I am . . . you know . . . bisexual.**

And her saying – snarling – sobbing – whispering – kissing my hand as she clung to me – bargaining with me desperately

And me saying –

She changes her mind.

– no, sorry. You don't get that. You don't get to see that.

. . .

I think I'll skip the rest. It was ugly and boring, like all break-ups are. I don't want to give you the wrong idea, she was so angry at her brother, furious, it was – terrifying actually. But she never quite seemed surprised by any of it. He was her brother, after all.

There is a funny little coda to all this – well, not funny ha ha. I go back to work quite quickly afterwards because – because I hope rather than think I can just carry on – and Shauna sends me the email with links to all the things I have to tweet about. **Focus on LGBTQ+ this week,** it says. I skim: celebrating LBT board members and staff, trans-inclusive policy, did you know bisexual women are significantly more likely than both heterosexual and lesbian women to have experienced partner abuse. Nearly five times more likely to have been sexually assaulted. Higher levels of mental illness, self-harm, suicidal ideation, drug and/or alcohol dependency, and intimate partner violence. Significantly worse for bisexual women who are women of colour, disabled, and/or trans.

And there it is, in black and white. I go into the kitchen, and as the kettle boils, I watch the red vines growing and I feel my pulse stirring. Miriam found me sobbing over a mug of instant coffee and she held my hand in silence for a while.

Because it's in me now. As I talk to you, I can feel the lick of vines curling around my wrists, and when I leave this place, things that blossom will follow me and shade me as I go. The forest will take over the house, the branches will come out of the windows, the trunks vanish down through the floors, the roots crack the foundations. I could have built a house from my body for her, let the timbers of my ribs hold us close. One day I still will. For someone.

Spring again. I brush my leaves out of my eyes, and scratch the bark behind my ear. Amber climbs the walls of me. I am flesh and breath, cambium and heartwood, foliage and hair, teeth, vein, sap, plasma, skin and resin, pulse and pulse and pulse.